KIDS THROUGHOUT HISTORY™

Kids During the Industrial Revolution

Lisa A. Wroble

The Rosen Publishing Group's
PowerKids Press™
New York

Published in 1999 by The Rosen Publishing Group, Inc.
29 East 21st Street, New York, NY 10010

First Edition

Book Design: Danielle Primiceri

Photo Credits: Cover, pp. 4, 7, 11, 12, 15 © Archive Photos; pp. 8, 16, 19, 20 © Corbis-Bettmann

Wroble, Lisa A.
    Kids during the industrial revolution / by Lisa A. Wroble.
        p.   cm.—(Kids throughout history)
    Includes index.
    Summary: Discusses the social and economic climate of the industrial revolution as it pertained to the life and daily activities of children.
    ISBN 0-8239-5254-1
    1. Industrial revolution—United States—Juvenile literature. 2. Children—United States—History—Juvenile literature. 3. United States—Social conditions—To 1865—Juvenile literature. [1. Industrial revolution—United States. 2. United States—Social conditions—To 1865. 3. United States—Social life and customs.] I. Title. II. Series: Wroble, Lisa, A. Kids throughout history.
HC105.W76 1998
305.23'0973'09034—dc21   97-43165
                                                                          CIP
                                                                          AC

Manufactured in the United States of America

Contents

Changing Times

The **Industrial Revolution** (in-DUS-tree-ul rev-oh-LOO-shen) was a period in history from 1650 to about 1890. It began in England. By the 1700s, it had spread to Belgium, France, and Germany. In the 1780s, it arrived in America. Revolution means a time of very fast change. Sometimes war brings about these changes. But this was not the case for the Industrial Revolution. The use of machines changed the way people worked. Cities began to grow. This also changed the way people lived.

Many families moved from farmland in the country to the city during the Industrial Revolution.

Machines and Factories

Many machines were invented during the Industrial Revolution. These machines could do the work of several men. Before machines, families had to work together to grow food. Everyone helped make what was needed. But machines did these things faster. They **manufactured** (man-yoo-FAK-cherd) things better than people could. Factories were opened that had many machines which made all kinds of things. Factory owners needed people to operate the machines. So farm workers moved to the city. They hoped to get jobs that paid higher wages.

Many big factories were built during the Industrial Revolution. ▶

Millwork

The first factories were called mills. They were built next to rivers. Big water wheels were turned by the river. This powered the machines. Mary Engel's family left their farm to move near a **textile** (TEK-styl) mill in New England. Both her parents worked at the mill. But their family needed more money for food and rent. At the same time, the mill needed small children to work there. Smaller kids were able to fit beneath the **looms** (LOOMZ) to sweep and to tie broken threads. Soon Mary and her brother went to work at the mill.

◄ *Children always found work in mills because their small fingers were just right for fixing the thread on the looms.*

9

The Industrial City

As more people came to work in the factories, cities began to grow around them. Workers lived near the factories so they could walk to and from work. The factory soon became the center of the city. The steam engine was invented in 1720. With this invention, factories did not need to be near rivers anymore. Unlike mill machines, steam-engine machines used coal as **fuel** (FYOOL) for power. More and more factories were built. Smoke from the steam engines clouded the air. People and houses crowded the cities.

Big steam engines like this made work easier, but they also made the air dirtier. ▶

Tenements and Row Houses

Many houses were squeezed into the spaces between factories. All of these homes were small and dark. Some of them didn't even have electric lights or running water. Since the walls of one house touched the next, they were called row houses. Mary's family lived in a row house. Her friend Eileen lived in a **tenement** (TEN-uh-ment). A tenement was like one row house stacked on top of another. Eileen lived on the third floor. She had to climb many stairs to reach her home.

◀ *Many people who worked in the factories lived in crowded tenements.*

Making and Sending Goods

Life in the factories was about making goods. Each factory made different things. Mary's textile mill was a factory that made cloth. Her father packed up the cloth so it could be sent to cities all across America. Big steam-engine trains were invented in the 1800s. They carried goods to the West and to the cities in the South. Certain things, like food, also had to be brought into the city where Mary lived. There was simply no room in an industrial city to grow food.

Steam-engine trains made it easier to send goods to many different cities. ▶

Food

The use of steam-engine trains changed what kinds of food people ate. People in the East and North could now get fresh vegetables in the winter. This was because the growing season was longer in the South and the West. Fruit and fresh meat could be enjoyed all year round rather than just in the summer. But Mary's family could not always afford fruit and meat. Her family bought a lot of potatoes and grain. These things could be stored longer than fruit or meat. Mary's mother would make bread and **porridge** (POR-ij) with the grain they stored.

◀ *People could enjoy food from all across the United States because of steam-engine trains.*

Clothing

Mary's family made cloth at the mill, but they never bought any. They could not afford it. Instead, the family wages were used to pay rent on their row house and to buy food. So shoes and clothing had to last a very long time. Holes in Mary's dress and her brother's pants and shirt had to be patched. When they went to work in the factory, Mary and her brother both wore sturdy boots on their feet and cotton aprons called smocks.

Kids who worked in factories often wore smocks to protect their clothes from getting dirty or torn. ▶

No Time for School

Mary wanted to go to school as she had when her family worked on the farm. But there was no time for school. At the mill, everyone worked twelve hours a day. **Whistles** (WIS-ulz) woke the workers at five o'clock in the morning. By six o'clock, they were working at the machines. When the workers got home in the evening, it was dark outside. They were all very tired.

Sunday was the only day the Engels did not work. Instead, the family went to church. After church, Mary and her brother were sometimes too tired even to play.

◄ *Even the kids who worked in the factories had to get up very early in the morning for work.*

Changes for the Better

A lot of people saw how hard Mary and other children worked. They knew this was unfair. They knew that children should not have to work long hours. Instead, kids should be able to go to school before getting jobs. People fought to make changes in the factories to protect children and other workers. Many of these changes are still in place today. In fact, the Industrial Revolution has a lot to do with the way we live today. Most people still live in cities. And many things we use are still made in factories. But children are no longer working there. They are free to be kids.

Glossary

fuel (FYOOL) Something used to make energy, warmth, or power.

Industrial Revolution (in-DUS-tree-ul rev-oh-LOO-shen) A period in history when the way people lived and worked changed due to the invention and use of machines and factories.

loom (LOOM) A machine used to weave fabric.

manufacture (man-yoo-FAK-cher) To make something by hand or with a machine.

porridge (POR-ij) Grain boiled with water, like oatmeal.

tenement (TEN-uh-ment) A building with many floors and with many families living on each level.

textile (TEK-styl) Cloth.

whistle (WIS-ul) A tube that makes loud, high sounds when air is forced through it.

Index